I0471037

Building Your Network Business

by David Satterlee

 Daily Inspiration

 Proven Ideas from
Successful Leaders

 Getting from Sweat
to Sweet Success

 Everyone's Guide to
Living a Better Life

Praise for David Satterlee and
Building Your Network Business

"This [publication] is loaded with great ideas. I buy it in quantity and give it to every new distributor that I recruit."
—DW, National Manager

Do you know yourself and what will bring you joy, satisfaction and security in life? You don't *have* to be a marketing superstar and a network leader. But, if you want to get there (and even if you don't) this book is for you.

David just plain gets it. He demonstrates a high level of emotional intelligence and sees how we can improve ourselves while treating others with understanding and compassion. This book is more than a list of ideas for self-employed entrepreneurs; it can also be taken as a general guide for living a happier, more-effective life.

Also by David Satterlee:

Chum For Thought (essays)
Life Will Get You in the End (short stories)

Follow at:

SocioDynamics.org
@ChumForThought
facebook.com/david.satterlee

Graybear Publications
104 N Main St
PO Box 198
Dayton, IA 50530

Copyright © 2013 David Satterlee

All rights reserved, including the right to reproduce this book
or portions thereof in any form whatsoever. For permissions,
write to: Graybear Publications, PO Box 198, Dayton, IA 50530

First Graybear Publications trade paperback edition
July, 2013

ISBN-13: 978-1490450337
ISBN-10: 1490450378

CreateSpace Independent Publishing Platform

Dedicated to the successful leaders who have had the commitment to persist and the vision to share their stories and ideas with others.

With special appreciation to Dianna Satterlee who, among many other blessings, knows wingnuts and conjunctive adverbs when she sees them. Also, Joy E. Marshall, and her good friend CoudjaWoudjaWhen.

Table of Contents

This page was inadvertently left blank.

Who do I see about that?

Section 1 — Introductory Stuff

A little background

This book was reborn from the publication *Better Business Building* (BBB), which I wrote in 1996. I digested the available literature, but was especially blessed to collect the best ideas available from the most experienced managers.

BBB was targeted at distributors of a nutritional supplement multi-level marketing (MLM) company. ("Network Marketing" is now more politically correct in some organizations.) I formatted the text of BBB as a set of index cards which could be studied serially, browsed for ideas, or read one-per-day for inspiration.

Better Business Building was a lot of fun to write, and enthusiastically used and endorsed by Senior Managers. For this book, I have removed the company-specific information, updated the contents and formatted the information as a book.

It's all just food for thought

Some things work for some people but aren't right for others. Sometimes, the time is not yet right for you or your situation. Don't worry if something just doesn't feel right; put the idea aside for later or mark the page with your own ideas.

This guide is packed with clichés. Some people claim that clichés are trite and don't always apply. Those critics are throwing out the baby with the bath water. I think clichés are the distilled wisdom of our culture. So it's up to you; if the shoe fits, wear it; if it's not your ladder, don't climb it. This guide is also packed with quotes. For instance:

> "The words of truth are always paradoxical."
> — Lao Tzu

This information should help you find helpful ideas and consider your choices. But, *you* are the judge of the commitments that you accept and the choices that you make.

Be warned — don't start a business without deciding why you're in it. Are you looking for a way to earn a little extra cash? Help others to be healthier and happier? Become secure, successful and the leader that you always knew you could be? Any business, especially one like this, can change your life.

Ideas for using this guide

These pages do not have to be read in any particular order. I figure that some people will want to read them by type of idea while others will want to review them by personal priority or how well they apply to individual situations. You will probably have an even better idea.

This is not a good book to read straight through, just once, without pausing. I suggest that you read a little bit at a time. It's more like a collection of poems than a novel. Scan it first to see what's in it, read some of the pages that look interesting and then put it down for a little while. I hope that you'll end up reading the whole thing, but I've got a hunch that it will digest better in small bites, chewed carefully. You can:

- find new ideas for your own success and happiness.
- search for ideas for distributors who are having trouble.
- borrow ideas for your newsletters and business meetings.
- review a few paragraphs every night before sleeping and let your subconscious be thinking about it for you. Keep

a pen and paper beside your bed for when you wake up with a great idea.

If you see a good idea, use it.

"I see the better way, and approve it; I follow the worse."
— Ovid

Additional quotes on personal growth

"Change and growth take place when a person has risked himself and dares to become involved with experimenting with his own life."
— Herbert Otto

"Can it really be said that before the day of our pretentious science, humanity was composed solely of imbeciles and the superstitious?"
— R. A. Schwallerde Lubicz

"One way or another, we all have to find what best fosters the flowering of our humanity in this contemporary life, and dedicate ourselves to that."
— Joseph Campbell

"The heart has its reasons that the mind knows nothing of."
— Blaise Pascal

"Without love the acquisition of knowledge only increases confusion and leads to self-destruction."
— J. Krishnamurti

Spirituality

We should be aware of our spiritual need. Recognition of our relationship to our source of spirituality keeps us balanced and secure. For the worshipful, this respect and affection for the wisdom of our Creator makes us want to imitate His qualities and gives us appreciation for His creations.

Commitment

Commitment means that progress occurs over time and that you need to stick with your goals in order to achieve them.

> "Far away, there in the sunshine are my highest aspirations.
> I may not reach them, but I can look up and see their
> beauty, believe in them, and try to follow where they lead."
> — Louisa May Alcott

Courage

Fear is the little death that kills. We need not be consumed by the past. The past has, for better or worse, had its day and it is gone. The past is available for learning, but need not consume us. In every moment, all we can do is make the best choices that we can, in that moment, and move on. We need not be consumed by fear of the future. You can't control everything. Again, all that you can do can only be done just now. Do it with courage and move on.

> "Moral courage and character go hand in hand – a man of
> real character is consistently courageous, being imbued with
> a basic integrity and a firm sense of principle."
> — Martha Boaz

Conscience

When you do what you know is right, you are at peace with yourself. If you have done things that did damage you can offer whatever restitution you can, commit yourself to doing better next time and seek forgiveness from God, your neighbors and yourself.

> "Cowardice asks the question, Is it safe? Expediency asks the question, Is it politic? Vanity asks the question, Is it popular? But conscience asks the question, Is it right? And there comes a time when one must take a position that is neither safe, nor politic, nor popular, but he must take it because his conscience tells him it is right."
> — Martin Luther

Section 2 — Communicating

First impressions

First impressions count. Are you cheerful, clean and dressed appropriately? Don't you prefer to do business with someone who knows their job, wants to help and looks like they have respect for themselves and you, their customer?

What if you're taking lots of garlic for your health? Some people will understand but you run the risk of offending others. Strong body odors or bad breath will make it a lot harder for people to feel (or get) close to you.

Are you personable? That is, are you likeable and sincerely interested in the people you meet? If you come on like a tornado, expect people to scream and run. If your personality needs some work, it may take persistence, but change is possible.

Because you are promoting well-being, you should be

committed to getting healthy and looking healthy. Of course you may still be overcoming the serious (perhaps life-long or life-threatening) health problem that got you interested in better health in the first place. But, so far as it is within your power, set a good example. People will know if you are a hypocrite.

Have you checked your voice? Are you easy to understand? You need to speak clearly and smoothly. If your vocabulary is too limited or you use words inappropriately you may lose respect. The same thing goes if you use big words just to show off. These things can be fixed. Don't forget to smile!

Just ask

Irma helped create attendance at a nearby meeting by asking. Irma says that it was just a matter of extending an invitation. The people she brought would not have known to come without being asked.

You can do the same. More people than you know are interested in natural health and will be delighted to learn more. They will respond positively to your initiative. Whether you are inviting people to a meeting, asking them to join you as a distributor or just tell you the time, you can learn to get results.

Be prepared and know what you want. Write down a few notes if necessary. Be clear and direct when you ask. Your request has to be easy to understand. It needs to make sense. Can you offer a good reason for them to do what you ask? Will it help them get what they want in some way? Will you need to answer concerns or overcome objections?

It is best to be firm and direct. You will weaken your request if you use phrases such as "... don't you think?" or "Maybe I'm wrong, but...." On the other hand, if you're too pushy people will think that you are a bully or disrespectful. You want to be assertive, not aggressive. Use steady eye contact, a serious (but not negative) expression and a firm but friendly voice.

The purpose of many conversations is to make something happen. Don't forget to actually ask.

Take the time to listen

People are happy to find someone who is interested in them and willing to take the time to listen. Most modern medical professionals are anxious to make a quick diagnosis and are too busy to spend the time to really know their patients. And, they rarely take the time to teach their patients how to make the changes needed for better health. Are you willing to truly listen to your customers and clients?

Studies have shown that just having someone listen can reduce the number and severity of a person's health complaints! People really appreciate someone who is willing to give the gift of their time and attention. So commit the time that is needed to identify people's individual needs. When you are done, you will have made a friend as well as a customer.

Do you interrupt people? Are you impatient? If you suggest a solution before you finish hearing the problem, will that person take your advice? Are you so busy planning what you will say next that you don't really hear what they are saying? Your response could be way off base. Does your mind wander to other subjects? If so, your body language probably shows it.

"Constantly talking isn't necessarily communicating."
— Charlie Kaufman

Pay attention to the other person's background and frame of reference. It's a shame to get into an argument about words when you actually agree with each other.

Interactive listening

Effective listening is an interactive process. You don't just stare at someone's lips and try to memorize their words. If you care about understanding what the other person means, you have to get involved. This will show that you are interested and paying attention. Remember that you have two ears but only one mouth.

Encourage the other person to talk. Ask open-ended questions that can't be answered "yes" or "no." You might ask for clarification or additional information. You can show your interest by asking "how" or "why."

Short reflective statements create rapport and assure the speaker that you are understanding him. Reflective statements are especially helpful when dealing with emotions. For instance you might say, "So you're really worried that the neighbors will complain about our yard."

Sometimes you should paraphrase what you have just heard. This lets the speaker decide if your interpretation of their message was correct. By receiving feedback, they can provide additional explanation, if needed, to be assured that you understand. "Yes, the yard does need to be mowed by Friday." Paraphrasing, in summary, at the end of a long conversation, is especially important when decisions have been made. Be careful not to constantly interrupt by "interacting" too often.

Reading people

If you're going to read people you have make a deliberate decision to pay attention. In his book, *What They Don't Teach You at Harvard Business School*, Mark H. McCormack suggests:

Listen aggressively — Listen to what they say and how they say it. Pause and they will say more.

Observe aggressively — Notice their body language, dress and mannerisms.

Talk less — You will make fewer mistakes and you will hear more. Ask questions sincerely for more information.

Take a second look at first impressions — First impressions are generally good but step back and evaluate them when you have had the opportunity to get to know the person better.

Take time to use what you've learned — Before you meet again, take some time to review what you know about that person and anticipate probable responses.

Be discreet — Keep a poker face and don't blow your hand. Keep your opinions about them to yourself and don't nervously blurt out your own weaknesses.

Be detached — Mentally step back to observe a situation when it starts to evoke your emotions. Act with purpose rather than reacting impulsively.

Tell stories

Some of the world's finest experts will bore you to tears every time. So what if you know every detail of the marketing plan and can repeat it in detail? So what if you know all the properties of *carthamus tinctorius*? People don't want you to recite dry facts; they like to hear stories.

Pretend that you are the historian of a primitive tribe. There are no books, no infomercials and no movies; just you and your stories. Now you have to pay better attention. You have to remember what happened and you have to be able to repeat it to others. You are the story teller and everyone is waiting for you to tell a story.

Stories do more than transfer information. Stories reach the heart and trigger emotions. When you reach a person's emotions with your story you create the motivation to follow through with the knowledge that you associated with it.

Testimonials make good teaching stories. They tell of the triumph of good over evil and smart over stupid. They teach how people have used the power of earth and sun, of the Creator himself, to restore themselves and others to health. Stories motivate and inspire. Best of all, you don't have to wait until you become an expert to start learning and telling good stories in an interesting way.

> "Mutat nomine de te fabula narratur. — Change the name and it's about you, that story."
> — Horace."

Projecting passion

Passion is the sizzle of love in a presentation. It is enthusiasm for a cause. It is the natural consequence of explaining something you believe in deeply.

People recognize, appreciate and respond to genuine passion. They know you're not a fake. This kind of genuine confidence with happy enthusiasm is contagious.

To have passion for your products you must "own" them physically, mentally and emotionally. You've tried them, you know them and you love them!

Passion is best projected simply. It needs to be clear and to the point. It is childlike in its truthful simplicity. You'll say: "Just wait until you hear about ..."

Passionate people have personal stories to tell. Their enthusiasm comes from their personal experience. People love to hear stories. When people identify with your stories, they will buy your products to share the emotions of the stories associated with them.

> "Only connect! That was the whole of her sermon. Only connect the prose and the passion, and both will be exalted, and human love will be seen at its highest."
> — E. M. Forster

> "Passion, I see, is catching."
> — Shakespeare, *Julius Caesar*

Sincerity

People can tell when you are sincere. You really mean it. You care that you get it right. You care about the person you're talking to. People know when you are sincerely interested in them.

You do not have to be an expert to be sincere. You can know just what you know and share it with sincere interest. Sincerity is direct, simple, pure and personal. People recognize that you are just what you say you are; there is no attempt to hide anything or mislead them. If you are sincere, you are more likely to be accepted because people will perceive you as completely open, honest and without pretense.

Sincerity is increasingly difficult in this dangerous and cynical world. People expect others to "look out for #1" and know that they must "always watch their back." It may take them a while to recognize your innocence.

"The most awkward means are adequate to the communication of authentic experience, and the finest words no compensation for lack of it. It is for this reason that we are moved by the true Primitives and that the most accomplished art craftsmanship leaves us cold."
— Ananda K. Coomaraswamy

Your attitude toward customers

Your attitude shows through everything you do. Do you REALLY appreciate customers? What have you done to reward your customers? If you reward your customers, they will want to repeat the action that was rewarded!

Every point of contact with a customer is important. It is your opportunity to make that person glad that they risked doing business with you. Every phone call, conversation and friendly wave is a chance to reinforce your connections with your customer. If you want them to be your lifetime partners, you have to create and use every possible opportunity to show them how much you care.

Customers are not objects to be influenced so that you'll make a lot of money. The only people who respond to this approach are those who are greedy and willingly deceive themselves. How sad.

Always ask yourself, "How can I make him glad he talked to me? What is the unmet want?" Always ask your customers, "How am I doing? How can I serve you better?" Then, listen to the answers and change your approach for the better.

"The purpose of the whole (work) is to remove those who are living in this life from a state of wretchedness and lead them to the state of blessedness."
— Dante

How to answer the phone

Always answer with a smile. Some folks keep a mirror near the phone so they can check themselves quickly before answering to be sure that they're smiling.

Research has shown that even a forced smile changes your brain chemistry and opens the way to feeling good. On the telephone, the only thing your listener has to go by is your voice and, you can believe it, your smile affects your voice. "Don't lift the phone without it."

> "Let us always meet each other with a smile, for the smile is the beginning of love."
> Mother Teresa

While you're listening, think nice things about your caller like "good friend" "really sincere," or "I love people like this." Then when you're speaking your thoughts will change your voice's subtle tones and inflections to carry your emotions across along with your words.

One of my phone problems is frowning when I don't quite know the answer to a question or have to say "no." I really like to say "yes" and not disappoint anyone. When I frown, people seem to sense it and usually think I'm unhappy at them. Really, I'm unhappy with myself for not having the best answer right away. Ouch! I'm really trying to work on that.

Phone folks frequently

The telephone is a very effective communication tool. When you have something to say, just pick up the phone and get your message across. Your fire will cool if you procrastinate until the next time you happen to meet.

A letter or email may use a lot more time. It doesn't project emotion well and doesn't let you work things out on the spot. A phone call is almost as good as a personal meeting and saves a lot of wear and tear on your car. You can even imagine the hug in the warmth of the speaker's voice.

Have you sold a new product to someone? Make a note of it and call them back in a week to see how they're doing with it. Get their phone number from the check, if you have to, but try to keep track and follow up.

You can phone your best new prospects and distributors every day. They will eventually figure out that you really care about them and you seriously want them to succeed.

Return phone calls promptly. Missed opportunities may never be repeated. People call when they are ready to discuss what's on their mind. Of course, if you are not sitting by the phone, waiting for their call, they may miss you. Still, the sooner you can get back to them, the more likely you are to connect with them.

Keep business phone calls organized

You can waste a lot of time on the telephone. Conversations ramble and the minutes of your day can disappear forever. That may be fine if you are chatting socially with a friend who also enjoys chatting socially, but it's a poor format for a business call. Business calls should be more direct and efficient.

Make an outline of the things that you need to communicate to the person you are calling. Generally stick to the outline. Check items off your outline as you work them into the conversation. When you are done, thank them and say goodbye.

When someone calls you, you can still be organized. Prompt them for the important information. When you are done, say goodbye. (If you just HAVE to cut someone off to hang up on them, consider hanging up while you're the one speaking. *Nobody* hangs up on themselves; the call must have been cut off by accident.)

Of course, conversations also serve the purpose of building relationships. There is no need to be so "organized" that you are cold, analytical and unsociable. But, having a conversation is like dancing; when the music stops, it's time to sit down.

> "Whatever we conceive well we express clearly."
> — Nicolas Boileau-Despréaux

Write a letter (or email)

Sometimes a letter is the best way to get your most important messages across. A letter gives you the time to compose your thoughts. It lets you express yourself carefully and completely. It permanently documents your message. Both parties can go back and refer to their copies of a letter. A letter is more formal than a conversation. It commits you in detail.

Writing a letter can help you avoid making hasty commitments. If you have written something in haste or anger you usually have time to think about things overnight and rewrite or destroy a letter. *Always* sleep on it and review a letter the next day if you have anything negative or emotional to write. You'll thank yourself almost every time.

Just a quick note about electronic mail networks. E-mail is the most dangerous of all letters, especially when you're upset. The writer is usually not as careful to compose his thoughts or guard against hasty statements. You can't tell how the other person is responding and correct any misunderstandings. You press SEND, the message is on its way, it's too late to take it back, and you're on record in writing. ZAP!

Keep in touch

Good friends become that way by having things in common, especially sharing experiences in each other's lives. If they don't continue to keep in touch, their lives diverge because they no longer have as much in common.

If you want to keep business relationships close, you have to behave the same way a friend would: keep in touch. Tell them about your experiences and share theirs. Ask for help when you need it. Be encouraging when they need it. Share the latest news and share your feelings. Besides using the phone, send newsletters, clippings and samples by mail. Don't miss a trick.

I know of some leaders who phone several times a week and even several times a day for aggressive distributors who are really working hard.

Your efforts to keep in touch with your organization will help them to be strong, active and ready to support each other just like you support them.

Always follow up

If a thing is worth starting, it's worth finishing. There are so many good opportunities that come up. You would invest a lot to generate a good opportunity. But, if you don't follow up, the opportunity is lost. What a waste when you don't follow up on things. What if a farmer prepared his fields but never planted or he planted but never harvested?

It's so easy to start a conversation and get someone interested in your products or business opportunity. Now what? You go home and send them some clippings. Do you call to discuss the clippings? Do you invite them to a meeting? Do you recommend helpful books (like this one)?

Maybe one of your customers buys some nutritional supplements. Do you call after several days to see how things are going? They may need encouragement to get past the bad taste or a rash if they start cleansing. Do you call after several weeks to see if they are about out and ready to replenish their supply?

Maybe one of your distributors calls to ask a question. They're READY to progress another step. Do you call them back to move them further down the path?

> "Either do not attempt at all or go through with it."
> — Ovid

> "Do or do not. There is no try."
> — Yoda

> "You can't jump a chasm in two bounds."
> — Ancient Chinese proverb

Make meetings fun

Keep people interested and ready to come back to your next meeting. Make meetings fun by being upbeat and unpredictable. Offer prizes, food (good natural stuff, of course) and other incentives.

Product demonstrations can keep people involved. You can taste herbs to understand their action, show how fiber swells in water or compare aloe juice to competitors' products. There are all kinds of demonstrations. Ask around, experiment at home and watch for demonstrations at conventions for more ideas.

Terrie says, "When someone's attention seems to wander, I

try to get them personally involved. I make eye contact with them and sometimes directly ask their opinion." Terrie says that she has even thrown erasers at people during meetings when their attention wandered. Well, she admits that she only threw them at people who already know and love her, but it sure did keep everybody else on their toes!

You can encourage people to participate by asking them to do research on an herb or combination formula, and then present their information to the group.

Schedule a fixed amount of time for their part of the meeting. This will help them to know how much information to prepare and help them to not carelessly run too long. When people know that you're counting on them (tell them: "I'm counting on you!"), they will be more inclined to show up, be on time and increase their participation in other ways.

> "Be sincere, be brief, be seated."
> — Franklin D. Roosevelt, (Advice to his son, James)

Use company videos

A professionally-produced video is a good way to start meetings. They break the ice and quickly grab attention. Of course, people came to hear a real person, so you should use the video as a tool to generate interest in what you have to say, not as a substitute for you, your enthusiasm and your testimonials.

Company videos are usually professional and well-done. When people see them, they give you added credibility. People realize that you are associated with a very professional, progressive company. After you've talked for a while about products, you might use another video segment to explain the business opportunity.

Company videos are also a good way to train your successline. Consider holding regular business meetings that feature company training videos.

> "How am I supposed to learn surgery if I can't dissect anything?"
> — Calvin, *Attack of the Deranged Mutant Killer Monster Snow Goons*, Bill Watterson

Section 3 — A Small Business in the Family

Getting your husband's respect and attention

A common problem for married women who start a network marketing business is an over-protective husband. The guy may really believe that his wife is getting burned by a get-rich-quick scheme or that herbalists are all quacks. Of course, a few *cascara sagrada* (a stimulant laxative) brownies will loosen him up (pun intended) and convince him of the power of herbs. But seriously ....

Larry was really skeptical when his wife Maureen got into direct sales. He says: "It's a whole lot different than the typical direct sales company. The company is based on education and taking care of the people you sign up." Maureen patiently won him over. Now he adds: "I've got a couple of Managers who didn't get their husband's attention until they got nice bonus checks."

Once your husband notices how well you are doing, you're all set for the next most common problem. He'll want to dive in, take over and reorganize. Well, you wanted his attention ...

"Many individuals have, like uncut diamonds, shining qualities beneath a rough exterior."
— Juvenal

Getting respect from family and friends

Strangers will take you at face value. They will judge you quickly, but at least they will give you a moment's chance.

The people who already know you may be harder to convince that you have something new to say. They've already classified you as "mother of three," "computer nerd" or "Uncle Jake with the strange tattoo." These mental perceptions run deep. You may never convince your mother that herbs are wonderful or that you know what will help with her gout.

The key to breaking old patterns of perception is simply to exercise the consistency and persistence to make deep new patterns. As you continue to do your new thing, you will build a new reputation and your family and friends will have to start seeing you in a new light.

Involving your spouse

If your spouse doesn't share your enthusiasm, all is not lost. Managers who have seen it often say that it's not unusual for the reluctant spouse to eventually join the other in the business. But it usually takes time and the right attitude.

The best advice is to not push too hard; that would only alienate them and make life harder. If you're going to improve their diet, do it gradually. If you start them on an herbal program, choose one that is "just right" – one that will gently improve their health over time. Listen to their concerns and do what you can to not challenge them in that area. Show your spouse the respect they need in order to earn the understanding that you want.

Show that you still love and support your spouse. If you quietly and persistently keep on without in-your-face confrontations, your spouse can lower their defenses. Once that happens, you can involve them gradually, answer their questions and quiet their fears.

You're not going to take away everything they love to eat and force them to live on carrot tops and turnip greens. All you want is to contribute to the financial security of your family and help others in the process.

> "There is nothing so easy but that it becomes difficult when you do it reluctantly."
> — Terence

Involving your children

Helping in the family business can be one of the most significant constructive influences on the developing self-confidence of a young person. Instead of watching TV or playing video "virtual reality," here is a chance to experience real reality. They can develop real skills and feel very much needed and appreciated.

Your children can earn and save significant amounts of money. (You DO plan to pay them, don't you?) We promised our boys when they were in their early teens that we would match whatever they had saved to invest in their own cars, when the time came. Our youngest took that to heart and tucked his money away for several years. When the time came, we paid up several thousand dollars against his first car. He learned his lesson too well, but we were proud of his determination and good choices.

A child who learns to meet and talk to strangers, handle money correctly, make decisions and be responsible for the feeding the fish will already have what it takes to function away from home when they are more "grown up."

You can work out schedules that allow appropriate time for homework and other school activities, play time with friends and vacations. The biggest surprise benefit can be an improved bond between parents and the child at a time when they might otherwise be growing apart.

Certain product and marketing questions and situations come up regularly. Children really take pride when they can provide the right answer with authority. Of course, children don't know all the answers at first, but neither did you.

Living herbally ever after

In a nutritional supplement company, the natural health philosophy can seem pretty scary at first. It can run completely counter to strongly-held popular beliefs about nutrition and drugs. Your spouse may think you've joined a cult or taken one too many enemas. Maybe your new interest disrupts a comfortable routine and makes your family feel insecure or robbed of your attention.

Eventually something will happen that can change their mind. Gloria started her business as a hobby and got her husband Jim's attention when she won a free trip to Lake Tahoe. Gloria says: "He was so impressed all he could say was 'Wow!'"

When husband and wife share common values and goals, life is much more rewarding. Maybe you will have to give up your business to make peace in the family. Maybe your family will join you in the business. Either way, you will have learned how to be healthier so that you can "live herbally ever after."

Men, women and relationships

The women in my extended family started passing around and discussing the books by John Gray, Ph.D. This is the fellow who wrote *Men Are From Mars, Women Are From Venus.* A little more slowly, some of the men are catching on. Not surprisingly, the guys who have always been the most obnoxious pigs are having no part of it.

Dr. Gray has been counseling couples for over 20 years. He took his observations to workshops and seminars and then started writing books. He's clearly a keen observer of human nature and deserves your attention.

He writes about the obstacles to good communication between men and women. For instance, John explains that we all need love but a man tends to identify with his actions and responds best to trust, appreciation and acceptance while a woman tends to identify with her feelings and responds best to respect, understanding and care.

He says that men and women respond differently to stress. A man will tend to withdraw and become more focused to deal with stress; he needs to "go to his cave" to come up with a plan. A woman will tend to lose focus and overwhelm; she needs her man to listen as she shares her anxieties. These differences often provoke men and women into behaviors that are completely misunderstood by their spouses.

I recommend these books to anyone, in a relationship or not, who wants to improve their ability to understand, communicate and love.

Section 4 — Mastering the Vision Thing

Personality types — your approach to work

How do you interact with those around you? How do you see yourself? How do you resolve problems? If you understand these things about your personality, you can make more progress with less confusion. You will engage your creative energies consciously and constructively. Consider some typical psychological models:

Hero — The explorer, decision-maker, adventurer, leader, servant of humanity.

Showman — The entertainer, artist, master of perception, imaginative creator.

Warrior — The persistent achiever, master of focused concentration, craftsman; powered by aggressive energy.

Scholar — The eternal student, wise teacher, steward of knowledge, compassionate nurturer.

This is just a glimmer of the available information of personalities. The more you know about how people think and why they do the things they do, the better you can get along with others and the better you can be at persuading them to love your products and marketing plan.

> "Look within. Within is the fountain of good, and it will ever bubble up, if thou wilt ever dig."
> — Marcus Aurelius

Life and love as art

Life should be rich, full and satisfying. Life is our gift to enjoy. Life is our obligation to produce and serve. Life should be lived with style and grace; it is its own art.

When you create something, make it appealing as well as functional. Your extra effort is an act of love for yourself, your Creator and your community.

> "We have come to think of art and work as incompatible, or at least independent categories and have for the first time in history created an industry without art."

> "The vocation, whether it be that of the farmer or the architect, is a function; the exercise of this function as regards the man himself is the most indispensable means of spiritual development, and as regards his relation to society the measure of his worth."
> — Ananda K. Coomaraswamy

> "To love is to transform; to be a poet."
> — Norman O. Brown

> "The secret of art is love."
> — Antoine Bourdelle

> "The art of life, of a poet's life, is, [when] not having anything to do, to do something."
> — Henry David Thoreau

> "... a first-rate soup is more creative than a second-rate painting."
> — Abraham Maslow

The entrepreneurial personality

Do you have what it takes to run your own business? There

are some personality traits that are common to entrepreneurs.

A representative of the Kravis Leadership Institute at Claremont McKenna College in Claremont, California, explains about entrepreneurs:

"They have a high need for achievement.

They have a high tolerance for ambiguity and are comfortable adding their own structure to ambiguous situations.

They usually have a single vision they do not swerve from, and they believe they control their own destinies." *Entrepreneur*, February 1996, p. 30.

> "Your imagination is your preview of life's coming attractions."
> — Albert Einstein

> "I call intuition cosmic fishing. You feel the nibble, and then you have to hook the fish."
> — Buckminster Fuller

Decide to be a Sponsor/Manager

Anything less than achieving "manager" leadership level in a network marketing plan is haphazard. It's OK to be a distributor, but both the commitment and the rewards are limited. A manager accepts the responsibility to lead and support others. The big jump in responsibility (and financial reward) comes with being a manager. It takes planning to stay a manager.

The first step up the "ladder of success" is *deciding* that you *want* to be a manager. This is an important commitment. You want to start out well balanced and firmly committed. Once you begin climbing, and you take others along with you, your responsibilities increase. You will want to plan first and know what you need to do.

Learn how to become a manager. Go back and read the marketing plan brochure and the distributor manual. Ask your sponsor or their manager for advice. Follow their good example, or recognize and avoid their mistakes... and start looking for another mentor up the line.

Learn how to stay a manager. One company ran a statistical analysis of their computer records and found that managers with 10 or more active distributors rarely had problems staying managers.

> "No one knows what he can do until he tries."
> — Publilius Syrus

> "One comes to be of just such stuff as that on which the mind is set."
> — *Upanishads*

... and then you get letters ...

Once you have achieved "Manager" status, you'll realize that you certainly didn't do it alone. Your distributors will teach you more than you ever taught them. And, you'll get letters like this (real) one:

Dear [Manager],

I'd like to take the time to thank you for being a great manager and a good friend and for all of the good things I've learned from you. You are why I am where I am today. Last month I ranked 2nd among recruiters (Area Managers). I have 7 first line managers and 2 second line managers. I have been invited to Convention again this year, all expenses paid. My husband and I have been invited to [the president's] house for dinner next Saturday night and to a special photo session before the Awards Banquet. I am very excited but also overwhelmed by all of this. I still don't know why. I do nothing but educate my people and it just makes my organization grow. Again, I'd just like to tell you and [your spouse] ....

Thank You

Cast your bread upon the water

"Casting your bread upon the water" is a reference to the scripture at Ecclesiastes 11:1. It refers to the rewards of exceptional generosity. Bread is the "staff of life." When you are willing to part with something valuable, your generosity will be repaid. (As long as we're on the subject, compare Luke 6:38.)

Lillian from Bakersfield, California, says "Caring and giving genuine service is like casting bread upon the water: it always comes back. I just keep going at the business of helping people to better health, and I keep talking about the benefits of the business. There always seems to be people who want to hear more."

One of the most valuable things we have to share with others is our time and attention. Time is the stuff of which our lives are made. A beautiful thing about network marketing is that each sponsor benefits to the degree that they support the success of others.

> "He who would accomplish little must sacrifice little; he who would achieve much must sacrifice much; he who would attain highly must sacrifice greatly."
> — James Allen

Time: Use it or lose it

Every moment that is wasted is time you will never get back. So, take a moment to lock that into your consciousness.

You will have no trouble finding detailed information about time management and good organization. Then again, there comes a point where preparation ends and productivity begins.

Take advantage of every available opportunity to advance your purposes. Feel free to share your company philosophy with just about anyone you meet. Share your success with others and help to enrich their lives. They will never know that you have something valuable to share if you hesitate to let them know.

But life should never be *all* work. So, make time to relax and enjoy the rest that you have earned – and then get right back to work doing good and enjoying every minute of it!

"I was so full of sleep at the time that I left the true way."
— Dante

"*Sed fugit interea, fugit inreparabile tempus.* (But meanwhile it is flying, irretrievable time is flying.)
— Virgil

"Men talk of killing time, while time quietly kills them.
— Dion Boucicault, *London Assurance* (1841)

"No time like the present."
— Mrs. Manley, *The Lost Lover* (1696)

I see (I.S.E.E.) what I should do

Integrity — the things that you choose to do should not conflict with your best values. Your actions should have purpose and meaning. They should reflect the fact that you are responsible and honest.

> "Men acquire a particular quality by constantly acting in a particular way."
> — Aristotle

Service — Your actions should build up and create rather than destroy or take. Contributing to the welfare of others out of love will make you stronger and "make the world a better place."

> "Consciously or unconsciously, every one of us does render some service or other. If we cultivate the habit of doing this service deliberately, our desire for service will steadily grow stronger, and will make, not only for our own happiness, but that of the world at large."
>
> — Mahatma Gandhi

Enjoyment — When you find joy in doing what you love to do, your life will flow. Your creativity and enthusiasm will bring success. It is a gift that we can rejoice and do good and see good for all our hard work.

> "I enjoy life because I enjoy making other people enjoy it."
> — Tim Conway

Excellence — If it's worth doing, it's worth doing well. Why commit to doing something if you don't care enough about it to be persistent, determined and see it through to a satisfying conclusion?

"All labor that uplifts humanity has dignity and importance and should be undertaken with painstaking excellence."
— Martin Luther King, Jr.

Help for a hurting world

If your neighbor was lost and confused and you knew how to solve his problem, wouldn't you speak up? Who really is your neighbor? The world is filled with people who know that they're getting progressively less healthy. They are confused and frightened. They don't know where to turn and they don't like it. You can help. You've tried something that worked for yourself and your family and you can tell them about it.

At one convention, a Senior National Manager shared his philosophy with the attendees when he pointed out that: "There's a hurting world out there. Who is going to help them? If not me, who? If not now, when? If not, why?"

"Today … we know that all living beings who strive to maintain life and who long to be spared pain – all living beings on Earth are our neighbors."
— Albert Schweitzer

"When we quit thinking primarily about ourselves and our own self-preservation, we undergo a truly heroic transformation of consciousness."
— Joseph Campbell

"All work undertaken should be useful — not just for a day, or a year, but useful in the sense that it affords permanent improvement in living conditions or that it creates future new wealth for the Nation."
— Franklin D. Roosevelt

Draw a treasure map

If you haven't been somewhere before you may need good directions and a road map to get there. When you have a goal to reach, decide how you want to get there and plan your route ahead of time. Follow your map and you will find your treasure.

Verlyn tells distributors to map out a plan. "Draw a 'treasure map' - things you'd like to have or accomplish within one year's time. Don't quit until you accomplish them. Don't just dream... also have it come true! Decide you can do it, then do it with enthusiasm. If you can get on fire about what you are selling, others will feel your excitement."

We start from the foundation of our values. This allows us to develop a vision of where we want to go. When we commit to that vision, we have goals.

> "Values are nothing without action. Virtue is the goodness bound up in the actual demonstration of positive values."
> — David Satterlee

Next, we develop a strategy to guide us in achieving our goals. We commit to specific tactics; the things we must do next. If the things we do are truly consistent with our values, then we will be happy and feel productive.

> "Our plans miscarry because they have no aim. When a man does not know what harbor he is making for, no wind is the right wind."
> — Seneca

Section 5 — Getting it Done

Commit to goals — visualize the results

What do you want to achieve? Knowing your destination is a crucial step in getting there.

Written goals are best; they have real power. The act of committing your goals to paper forces you to clarify and refine them. Until you write it down, a goal is just a wish or a hope.

Tell people what you are planning to do. Now that someone else knows about your commitment, it makes it harder for you to break your implicit promise; someone will know.

If you want to improve the chances of someone keeping their commitment to you, get them to visualize doing what they've promised. For instance, ask them when they will leave, what route they will take and who they will bring with them. This kind of visualization helps to make their commitment more real in their mind.

Identifying goals actually reduces stress. Psychiatrists have discovered that helping their patients to establish personal goals is the most effective way to help them cope with problems. Establishing clear goals puts you in charge of your life.

A fixed goal, something that you can see clearly in your mind's eye, increases motivation; you can take the measure of your progress towards that goal. And, as you make progress, you will also anticipate the satisfaction of its completion.

> "In every block of marble I see a statue as plain as though it stood before me, shaped and perfect in attitude and action. I have only to hew away the rough walls that imprison the lively apparition to reveal it to the other's eyes as mine see it."
> — Michelangelo

> "A man's dreams are an index to his greatness."
> — Zadok Rabinowitz

Just don't do it

> "Work expands so as to fill the time available for its completion."
> — C. Northcote Parkinson, *Parkinson's Law*, (1958)

Parkinson wasn't being funny; he was dead-on serious. You've seen it happen. A perfectly reasonable job gets blown out of all proportion. It might be your fault. Or maybe the decision just had to be run back past a committee, which decided to form a sub-committee for further investigation.

If the task will produce a valuable return and it is straightforward and clear, consider just doing it. In fact, if someone asks you to do something, you agree that it is worth doing and you are at liberty to do it *right now*, why not go ahead? You will decrease the mental burden of a massive to-do list and seriously impress that person in the process.

On the other hand, tasks that can't be nailed down and done right away often grow into evil dragons. Ignore evil dragons; walk away from them and refuse to pay them any attention. Deny evil dragons; refuse to commit to things you don't really want (or have the time) to do. They will disappear and quit bothering you if just ignore them.

We can become so distracted by things that are urgent (but not important) that we end up spending all our time fighting fires, but not making real progress on important goals. It really is amazing how many really urgent, but actually trivial, things can simply be ignored without the world coming to an end. How wonderfully liberating!

Success isn't always easy

If you want to succeed at something truly worthwhile, be prepared for the struggle. Many have given up families, property and security in their homelands to pursue opportunity elsewhere. Many poor and disadvantaged have committed to making sacrifices to create desired changes in their circumstances or improve future opportunities for their children. The world's classic stories involve the struggle to overcome intimidating obstacles.

To succeed in any difficult endeavor we need to overcome fear and reach deep within ourselves for courage and determination. You may not be in favorable circumstances but there is always something more that you can try to improve your situation.

Have realistic time expectations. As an example, it can take about 10,000 hours across seven to ten years of persistent practice to *truly master* any profession, musical instrument, art, craft, sport, or business. Have you decided that your goal is worth achieving and that it is worth doing well?

> "Always bear in mind that your own resolution to succeed is more important than any other one thing."
> — Abraham Lincoln

> "Life shrinks or expands in proportion to one's courage."
> — Anais Nin

Sometimes, success is easy

Not everything is difficult or requires total mastery. There will also be things that will produce satisfactory results within the material and time resources that you have at hand. Don't be afraid to go have fun doing something worthwhile.

> "It is the greatest of all mistakes to do nothing because you can only do a little. Do what you can."
> — Sidney Smith

> "Do what you can with what you have, where you are."
> — Theodore Roosevelt

Have you noticed that sometimes events just seem to conspire to bless you? Is it just good luck or the random and unknowable nature of nature? You may believe in karma or a loving God who is looking out for your welfare. In any case, good things happen. Sometimes, good things happen a lot. When they do, it is a good time to have a "gratitude attitude," go with the flow, enjoy your blessings and share your bounty with others. Becoming a blessing to others just *has* to be a good thing.

Hard work

Hard work is needed to build a secure business. It can take extra hours each day and can require continued work over a span of years. But, it's easy to work hard when you love what you're doing.

Sometimes it happens that people begin coming from hundreds of miles away for help. When you can offer renewed hope and eventually, renewed health, it's hard to say "no." Your hard work can be a labor of love and service.

"Go the extra mile." This popular motto is a reference to Matthew 5:41. The point is to not be miserly with your commitments. When you hold back and only do something reluctantly you might as well have not done it; you only did what you were forced to do. If you are going to do something for someone else, give it all you've got. Do more than expected. This kind of behavior gets noticed and, in time, also gets rewarded. You'll feel good about yourself too.

Honesty and Integrity

Throughout recorded history, it has been a tendency of some men to set their own rules and do whatever seems best for themselves. "Business ethics" become especially loose with no hesitation to profit from the ignorance or misfortune of others, especially "if they are not of our own."

Some people worry that they will be at a financial disadvantage if they are not as "sharp" as their competitors. Others understand that people appreciate obvious integrity and prefer to do business with people who they like and trust.

Naturally, it's hard to enjoy the company of a thoughtless or ruthlessly selfish person. But, it works the other way round too. If you have cheated or taken advantage of someone, your conscience tries to justify itself by putting them outside of your favor; it is very hard to like them from that point forward. Bad relationships are death to a network marketing business.

> "Think nothing profitable to you which compels you to break a promise, to lose your self-respect, to hate any person, to suspect, to curse, to act the hypocrite, to desire anything that needs walls and curtains about it."
> — Marcus Aurelius

> "*Proprium humani ingenii est odisse quem laeseris.* (It is part of human nature to hate the man you have hurt.)"
> — Tacitus

Who is "we?"

As we grow and develop, our circle of inclusion should continue to grow as well. As young children, we barely distinguish ourselves from our environment; when our diaper is full, the whole world seems as unhappy as our own discomfort.

Later, we can recognize that there are other people, who can tell us what to do, give, take and punish. We begin to recognize others as separate individuals with emotions of their own that can be manipulated. Eventually, we may develop a capacity for full empathy for others. Some people continue to grow outward in their psycho-social capacities. What a blessing for the world!

As we develop, the scope of who we mean by "we" also expands. Babies and psychopaths only care about themselves. Later, we embrace our membership in families and close communities of friends and faith. We then think of those groups when we think of "we." Don't get me wrong here; family values are a wonderful thing. Belonging to a community group and having a faith that gives life meaning is good too.

But, development doesn't have to stop with "I'll do anything for my brother," or "My gang has to take care of itself." Many people feel better when their sports team wins or embrace the attitude "My country, right or wrong, my country."

But, being able to stand in front of another person with empathy for their background and problems allows you to treat them as brother or sister. If you want to be fully successfully in a personal service network business, it helps to be able to transcend blind racism or blind nationalism. It helps to be able to look at all humankind and think "we."

Dare to dream

Walt Disney's Cinderella sings: "A dream is a wish your heart makes." Would it have been better for Cinderella to have never seen the castle? Would she have been happier never knowing anything but the cinders?

Most times, we are so limited by what we think is practical that we don't see what is possible. Look up for a moment from the ground directly in front of you and see the world of possibilities all around you! You don't have to be daring to dream of improving your situation. In fact, if you never visualize a desired future, you cannot start to make it happen. Our dreams, hopes and aspirations are acts of faith. Faith moves mountains.

> "... faith is the substance of things hoped for, the evidence of things not seen."
> Hebrews 11:1, *King James Version*

Some people actually do live happily ever after. Why shouldn't you? Dare to dream. Exercise faith. Make it happen.

> "If you follow your bliss, you put yourself on a kind of track, which has been there all the while waiting for you, and the life that you ought to be living is the one you are living."
>
> — Joseph Campbell

Set outrageous goals

If you are going to dream, why not dream big? Miracles happen. Outrageous challenges have a special mystique and have the potential to generate unusual success.

- Impress yourself with dramatic results.
- Amaze your friends.
- Pump up your determination to do the unusual.
- Focus on a single goal.
- Keep that goal constantly in front of you.
- Put up signs and stickers everywhere to remind yourself.
- Infect everyone with your enthusiasm.

"Life is either a daring adventure or it is nothing."
— Helen Keller

"Whatever you can do, or dream you can, begin it. Boldness has genius, power, and magic in it."
— Goethe

"Never doubt that a small group of thoughtful, committed citizens can change the world; indeed, it's the only thing that ever has."
— Margaret Mead

Preparation + Opportunity = Advancement (make your own luck)

Some people always seem to have the worst luck. Sometimes, refrigerators really do fall out of the sky. But, most of the time, not being ready means that people don't even notice opportunities when they happen. Or, they go charging blindly into every quick-gratification scheme they see, getting disillusioned, and abandoning their investment.

Other people seem to have the knack for making their own good luck. It helps to have already thought about what you stand for and where you want to go next. Then, when the right door opens to you, you won't need to hesitate to step through. Preparation seems to have a way of attracting opportunities. Without preparation, you are not in a position to take advantage of opportunities even if you recognize them.

Opportunities ARE available. Some just seem to fall out of the sky. Others will wander by when you least expect them. But, they may not wait around for you. You may have to already have your resources (and willingness to commit them) ready. Then, when the right opportunity comes, just reach out and grasp it.

Or, you may have to just start digging and create your own opportunities. In any event, this boldness to advance seems to create a momentum toward success. Some people will just envy your good luck.

> "Until one is committed there is always hesitancy, the chance to draw back, always ineffectiveness. Concerning all acts of initiative (and creation), there is one elementary truth, the ignorance of which kills countless ideas and splendid plans: that the moment one definitely commits oneself, then Providence moves too. All sorts of things occur to help one that would never otherwise have occurred. A whole stream of events issues from the decision, raising in one's favor all manner of unforeseen incidents and meetings and material assistance, which no man could have dreamt would have come his way."
>
> — W.H. Murray, Member of the Second Himalayan Expedition

Keep on keeping on

Some people just seem to have trouble with everything they try. When things don't seem to be working out fast enough, they give up and try something else. The problem is that by not sticking persistently to any one thing, they consistently discard their efforts by moving on too soon.

> "Nothing in this world can take the place of persistence. Talent will not; nothing is more common than unsuccessful people with talent. Genius will not; unrewarded genius is almost a proverb. Education will not; the world is full of educated derelicts. Persistence and determination alone are omnipotent. The slogan "press on" has solved and always will solve the problems of the human race."
> — Calvin Coolidge

Jonas, a National Manager, explained his formula for success. "Keep on keeping on. The world will make room for the man who knows where he is going." He explained: "If I could give the reason for our success, I could do it with just a couple of words: consistent persistence. Line upon line. Precept upon precept. There's no formula to guarantee success in a few months' time. You have to keep with it. We're very excited about our business, and that helps others get excited."

> "There's no substitute for hard work."
> — Thomas Edison

> "Do not turn back when you are just at the goal."
> — Syrus

Doing the right thing before

I am, at core, a talented problem-solver. Let me offer a couple of pieces of my best advice:

1) Before setting out to answer a question, be sure that this is, in fact, the right question.
2) Before setting out to solve a problem, be sure that this is, in fact, the right problem.

No amount of faith, hard work, commitment, or persistence serves for good unless you are moving in the right direction. Have you engaged both your heart and your head? Did you do your due diligence and make sure that this was a good idea?

Fixing mistakes

"Everything we enjoy in society is a direct result of the accumulated learning derived from millions of mistakes. No mistakes, no progress. Yet we still look at making a mistake as embarrassing, wrong, an act bordering on sin. If you're making mistakes, it means you're doing new things, taking risks, stretching yourself. You're growing, learning."
— Robert White

When you make a mistake, fix it and move on. And, be kind to others when they make mistakes. I remember a story about the head of a major corporation being urged to fire a vice-president for failing to make a profit on a $150 million investment. A factory had to be closed and the employees there had to be let go. The president responded, "Why should I fire him? I just invested $150 million in his education."

Some stubborn, self-referential people can't learn from mistakes. You may have to drop them as friends or business associates. Lord help them. If you're one of those thoughtful, introspective people who can actually learn from the mistakes of others, you are already enjoying many blessings.

> "The first time you make a mistake, it's just a mistake. The second time, it's carelessness. After the third time, I assume that it's your philosophy."
> — Ronan Graybear

Doing the right thing after

There will come times when you realize that what you are doing no longer seems to make sense; it no longer has meaning or value to you. Change happens. It can be a good thing.

When you discover that you are doing the wrong thing, just stop. Sometimes it will be a real struggle to understand what the right thing is, but don't give up and don't just go carelessly back to the old known-and-familiar. You want to be doing the right thing, don't you? Even if it requires change?

Sometimes you just need to make a tactical change; like choosing to ride a different horse. This is called lateral movement or translation. These choices may be important and difficult, but they are relatively easy to get past.

On the other hand, personal growth demands that you will run into situations that are not explained by your present worldview. Personal development calls on you to make strategic changes that transcend your previous way of thinking; they move you vertically. Transcending your present limits and discovering your next level of worldview is a real challenge.

When you have successfully completed your struggle you will have a larger, more detailed understanding of what's happening and why. Your life will never be the same, but that's probably a good thing. Congratulations.

Section 6 — Coping with Fear, Risk and Crisis

The people keep you going

Most of us are in this business because we respect natural health. Mental health is a key part of our overall (natural) health. A well-recognized sign of strong mental health is creative service to others and freedom from selfishness. Such selfless service supplies a sense of calm satisfaction which further reinforces health. This positive cycle just keeps on going.

One of the beautiful elements of network marketing is the fact that people help people up and down the line. They not only have the satisfaction of helping others, but they actually are helping themselves in the process.

"It was never pushing this business that got us where we are today – it was helping others," says Marge. "We don't set goals; we help people. It's the people, including our wonderful Managers, that make you successful. You couldn't be in this business if you didn't give from the heart. The only thing that keeps you going is the people."

> "The power of man's virtue should not be measured by his special efforts, but by his ordinary doings."
> — Blaise Pascal

Handling rejection

Imagine that someone walks up to you and says: "You are a quack and a crook. You are unworthy of my attention. I'm not interested and I want you to go away." Yikes! What a nasty thing to read! Are you okay? Take a moment, if you need, to put yourself back together. The rest of this page will help.

When you make your emotions and convictions public, you can face some pretty personal assaults. Be prepared for this by having full faith in the value of your message. Then if (no, *when*) someone disrespects that message, you can bounce back. You can "shake the dust off your sandals" and move on.

Actually, rejection is no big deal. We expect a certain percentage of people to be so locked into their own ruts that they just can't see beyond their habitual ways of thinking. Your message may represent a threat to their precious, comfortable rut. They would have to make a change if they took you seriously.

On the bright side, maybe you gave them something to think about and their attitude will soften. It has happened. Then, when they come back seeking you out, your joy is doubled.

Rejection is, in fact, the natural environment of any marketing effort. Your message and style matter. But, in the end, the more often you put your message out there, the more rejections you will receive and the more positive responses you will collect.

Rejection is simply the way you know that it's time to move on. You will find so many kind and appreciative people that you will not even worry about those who are indifferent, ignorant, or rude. As you keep on, your pleasure and satisfaction keeps on growing and growing.

> "Every great movement must experience three stages: ridicule, discussion, adoption."
> — John Stuart Mill

Overcoming fear

What frightens you? Disapproval? Failure? You can take

your failure by fear all at once or in little bits. You have heard of people who have been so afraid of a shadow that their fear brought on a heart attack. Could they have had more mental control?

Fear can lead to inaction, indecisive action or wrong action; these all can hurt you. Texas roads are littered with dead armadillos and squirrels. Armadillos will stop still in the road. Squirrels will dash madly back and forth, unable to decide which way to run. Either way, their inability to move decisively leads to the same end.

I have known people who give in to their fear, bit by bit, until they are unwilling to leave their houses. I have known others who dash from one get-rich idea to another without pursuing one long enough to benefit from their efforts. Could they have had more mental control?

A key to overcoming fear is to want something strong enough that you are finally willing to plunge ahead despite your fears. Once you decide to act, you can redirect the energy of your fear into unexpectedly decisive action.

> "Has fear ever held a man back from anything he really wanted, or a woman either?"
> — George Bernard Shaw

> "Courage is not the absence of fear, but rather the judgment that something else is more important than fear."
> — Ambrose Redmoon

> "Let me not pray to be sheltered from dangers but to be fearless in facing them. Let me not beg for the stilling of my pain but for the heart to conquer it."
> — Tagore

"His flight was madness: when our actions do not, Our fears do make us traitors."
— Shakespeare, *Macbeth*

"We have nothing to fear but fear itself... nameless, unreasoning, unjustified terror which paralyzes needed efforts to convert retreat into advance."
— Franklin D. Roosevelt, First Inaugural Speech

"I believe that anyone can conquer fear by doing the things he fears to do ..."
— Eleanor Roosevelt

"Fear always springs from ignorance."
— Ralph Waldo Emerson

"Nothing is terrible except fear itself."
— Francis Bacon

If your friends and family don't understand

It can be discouraging if your friends don't understand why you are "doing this strange thing." You have a choice. You can fearfully give in to their ignorance or you can boldly persist in educating them.

For many years, I just deep down solid didn't get it. My wife would try to tell me about herbs but it didn't make sense so it irritated me. I wouldn't eat anything that was "good for you" and I certainly wouldn't take any capsules! Eventually it began to make sense and I changed. Give folks some time to adjust.

"Keep away from people who try to belittle your ambitions. Small people always do that, but the really great make you feel that you, too, can become great."

— Mark Twain

"Don't listen to friends when the Friend inside you says 'Do this.'"

— Gandhi

Risk = Commitment (Burning your bridges)

Have you heard the story of the explorer who burned his boats upon reaching the far land? His troops then had no option but to stay. They were irrevocably committed.

I operated my network business part-time for years and never grew much beyond the minimum sales required to stay a basic manager. When I gave notice to my employer, however, there was no turning back and I *really* paid attention to product sales and recruiting. When I put more at risk, I generated commitment.

"I have learned this at least by my experiment: that if one advances confidently in the direction of his dreams, and endeavors to live the life which he has imagined, he will meet with a success unexpected in common hours."
— Henry David Thoreau

"There are costs and risks to a program of action, but they are far less than the long-range risks and costs of comfortable inaction."
— John F. Kennedy

"Only those who risk going too far can possibly find out how far one can go."
— T. S. Eliot

Crisis time: excuse or challenge?

The Chinese pictogram for "crisis" is said to be composed of the symbols for "danger" and "opportunity." People tend to resist change but when a crisis strikes, change forces itself on you. Your only choice is how to react.

A crisis can be your excuse for feeling sorry for yourself and quitting. Maybe a natural disaster wiped out your home and business. Now what do you do? You could lose heart and quit. The other option is to simply start over and rebuild with what you have left. You may not have much, but you still have your integrity, drive and experience. You can be determined to do an even better job this time. When the universe hands you an opportunity, take it.

"Prosperity doth best discover vice, but adversity doth best discover virtue."

"A man must make his opportunity, as oft as find it."

"A wise man will make more opportunity than he finds."

"Chiefly the mould of a man's fortune is in his own hands."
— Francis Bacon

"When life gives you lemons, you don't make lemonade. You use the seeds to plant a whole orchard - an entire franchise! Or you could just stay on the Destiny Bus and drink lemonade someone else has made, from a can."
— Anthon St. Maarten

Revisiting failure

Try to not agonize over your failures. But, you should dwell on them. Think about what happened and why it went wrong. When you understand why you failed, you free yourself to try again.

History is full of inspiring stories of those who failed repeatedly but kept on trying again until they were successful beyond any expectation. I always think of Thomas Edison trying thousands of materials for the filament for his new electric light bulb. Although people seem altogether too happy to remind us of our failures, I really believe that some failures are evidence that you are out there doing something. Just don't keep on making the same mistakes.

"You only fail when you fail to try," according to Dr. Daniel Litchford, who was the motivational speaker at a New Managers' Convention. He taught: "I'm not judged by the number of times I fail, but by the number of times I succeed. And the number of times I succeed is in direct proportion to the number of times I fail and keep trying."

> "There is nothing left to you at this moment but to have a good laugh."
> — Anonymous Zen master

When you do wrong

Does it seem that today's business ethics favors the sharp operator while no one notices or punishes all the little dishonesties that people commit? Don't believe it. When we act from bad motives, it usually catches up to us. When we are greedy, selfish or covetous, the stream of good that was refreshing us just seems to dry up.

A manager from California, urges others: "Don't do anything you know is wrong or later you will feel sorry and it will affect your energy, your business. If you make mistakes, don't let them get you down; keep trying and you will do very well!"

If you realize that you are doing wrong, the best course is to turn it around as quickly as you can. Admit the wrong, ask forgiveness, repay or repair the damage that you have caused, forgive yourself and move on.

> "How pleasant it is, at the end of the day, No follies to have to repent; But reflect on the past, and be able to say, That my time has been properly spent."
> — Jane Taylor, *Rhymes for the Nursery. The Way to be Happy.*

> Forgiveness does not change the past but it does enlarge the future.
> — Paul Lewis Boese

If you say it, you have to do it

Isn't it funny? You can convince yourself that you really want to do something but you still put it off indefinitely. As long as you keep your goal private, it's just too easy to procrastinate.

The cure is to make your goal public; then you must follow through or else "lose face." Once you have made a public commitment, you feel a real obligation to begin, and then to keep your promise.

You might use public commitment to strengthen your decision to lose 15 pounds or to send out a monthly newsletter. When people ask you how much weight you've lost or want to know when they'll receive your next newsletter, you will be more likely to get back to work in order to meet their expectations.

The hardest part of any task is getting off to a good start. Once you actually get started, it's easier to keep going.

> "The beginning is the most important part of the work."
> — Plato

> Confidence... thrives on honesty, on honor, on the sacredness of obligations, on faithful protection and on unselfish performance. Without them it cannot live.
> — Franklin D. Roosevelt

Section 7 — Self Improvement

If it is to be, it's up to me!

Jack, of Bakersfield, California, endorses the motto: "If it is to be, it's up to me!"

If you fail to act, things will gradually come apart. Your plow will rust, termites will devour your walls and your distributors will lose interest. It is a universal law that things will become increasingly disorganized if left alone. Thus, we all have a responsibility to continuously invest our intelligence and creative energy into making things more organized. So, if you want something to happen, get out there, plan, invest your time and energy and take responsibility to make it happen.

> "But then if I do not strive, who will?"
> — Chuang Tzu

"Anyone who proposes to do good must not expect people to roll stones out of his way, but must accept his lot calmly, even if they roll a few more upon it."
— Albert Schweitzer

How to test your motives

The ideal motive for running your network business is to provide service to others. You may draw your faith in this principle from the teachings of Jesus or the concept of Karma, but the principle is sound. The trick is to not presume to anticipate repayment at the time you are performing an act of service.

Sometimes, however, your life situation puts a lot of pressure on you. Many of the people who are moved to begin a network business do so because they already have financial problems and need money now. This makes it very hard to avoid visualizing their neighbor's product purchase as their children's school shoes.

If this is your situation, do what you must from the need to do it. Relief from poverty by earnest endeavor is an honorable motive and most people will respond kindly to your hard work and good faith. (And you may just introduce them to the business opportunity that they need to solve their own problems.)

The real problems of motivation are with those people who see network marketing as their ticket to riches through the work of others. They are shameless, pushy and shallow. There's nothing wrong with looking forward to earning a car allowance or an Achievement Trip. But, if you spend all your time dreaming about retiring early and how important you'll look in your fancy yacht, then that's just shallow.

"It is preoccupation with possessions, more than anything else, that prevents us from living freely and nobly."

— Bertrand Russell

Happiness lies not in the mere possession of money; it lies in the joy of achievement, in the thrill of creative effort.
— Franklin D. Roosevelt

Know thyself

I've known some people who are an emotional mess. They don't understand themselves and they don't understand anyone else either. They don't know what they want out of life; they cast around randomly and unsuccessfully for affection, approval and control. They change jobs and spouses; nothing seems to make them happy. They may live dangerously to feel "alive" or they may resort to chemicals to hide from their desperate emptiness.

Knowing yourself not only means understanding your values and needs, but also having mastery of your goals, emotions and relationships. When you know what good things bring you a sense of satisfaction and purpose, you can invest your life cultivating, harvesting and distributing that goodness.

"Thoroughly to know oneself, is above all art, for it is the highest art."
Theologia Germanica

"To know oneself, one should assert oneself."
— Albert Camus

"It is never too late to be what you might have been."
— George Eliot

"Being in business is not about money. It is a way to become who you are."
— Paul Hawken

The pleasures of dedicated work

There is nothing like dedicated, focused attention to make things flow. Somehow, when you get completely involved, time seems to stand still and everything gets easier. It's like all the circuits in your brain line up to keep you on track. In fact, being fully absorbed in work is a distinctly pleasurable state of mind.

"When you are in the state of *flow*, you know that what you need is possible to do, even though difficult, and the sense of time disappears. You become completely focused in your activity. You forget yourself. You feel part of something larger."
— Mihaly Csikszentmihalyi, Psychologist

"Happiness lies not in the mere possession of money; it lies in the joy of achievement, in the thrill of creative effort."
— Franklin D. Roosevelt

According to a manager in Texas: "It's easy if you are willing to work hard and if you have the desire to achieve. It's difficult if you aren't dedicated to the work and the company. When I decided to dedicate myself full-time to [my network] business, it became much easier for me to achieve my business goals. The very reason I've worked all these years with the same endeavor is because I enjoy helping people find natural answers to their dietary concerns and talking about health and nutrition with them in words they are comfortable with and can understand."

"When you are inspired by some great purpose, some extraordinary project, all your thoughts break their bounds: Your mind transcends limitations, your consciousness expands in every direction and you find yourself in a new, great and wonderful world. Dormant forces, faculties and talents become alive, and you discover yourself to be a greater person by far than you ever dreamed yourself to be."

— Patanjali

Approval and control

What are the things that you really, down deep, want in life? Almost anything you can think of boils down to some form of approval or control. That makes the desire to feel approved and in control the most powerful influence for good (or bad) in our lives.

My sponsor urged me to learn to "release" on my desires for approval and control. She explained that they bound me to the responses of people who weren't even aware of their influence. In addition, these emotions especially bound me to manipulative people who had no personal interest in my welfare.

While discussing competition, my wife told me that while women compete for approval, men compete for control. Have you noticed that tendency? You can use that information to communicate better with the people you talk to.

"The hook is your desire to be approved by others. The bait is any kind of reward. The minute you go for the bait, the game is playing you. You are no longer playing the game. You get serious."

— Laurence G. Boldt

Waiting 'till later — the classic negator

"I'll do it tomorrow." — "Tomorrow never comes."

Be careful to not say "tomorrow" when you really mean "not today." Procrastination is the perfect way to put something off forever. It negates your good intentions. The best way to fight procrastination is do things right away. There's no time like the present. The second best thing is to keep a well-managed task plan.

Setting deadlines helps you to avoid being forced to rush at the last minute. Try to finish your monthly goals during the first 2 weeks. Place your orders early.

> "We take no note of time, but from its loss."
>
> "Procrastination is the thief of time."
> — Edward Young

> "To be contented is noble, but to be lethargic does not enable one to benefit men or to utilize things."
> — Hung Tzu Ch'eng

> "Tomorrow is another day."
> — Scarlet O'Hara, *Gone With the Wind*

Buy some flowers

Show your appreciation. Buy some flowers for someone who needs an emotional lift or needs to be reminded that you care. Flowers are truly special. They convey a sense of special tenderness and friendship. Buy some flowers for yourself too. You deserve it. You've been working hard and doing well. Take charge of brightening your own day and giving yourself a lift.

> "Flowers always make people better, happier, and more helpful; they are sunshine, food and medicine for the soul."
> — Luther Burbank

You don't have to limit yourself to flowers, of course. There are so many ways to show your appreciation! Search constantly to find ways to brighten someone's day. At Hewlett-Packard Company an engineer burst into his supervisor's office to announce that he'd solved an important problem. The manager groped in his desk for some way to give an immediate reward and came up with the banana from his lunch. The "Golden Banana Award" is now one of the highest honors an HP employee can receive.

> "The best portion of a good man's life – his little, nameless, unremembered acts of kindness and of love."
> — William Wordsworth

> "The only way to have a friend is to be one."
> — Ralph Waldo Emerson

Looking good

The most important part of looking good is a smile born of genuine happiness. Inner beauty always brings out the best in people. It is not necessary to have the finest clothes or perfect hair and makeup, but your attitudes will affect your appearance.

Respect for yourself and others demands keeping clean and being "presentable." I don't know which comes first, self-esteem or dressing well, but they do seem to reinforce each other. My great grandparents used to put on their better clothes when they left the house. It was a matter of respect for themselves and others. People today seem to want to be more "casual" but that is no excuse for being unkempt. Mary Kay Ash (chairman of Mary Kay Cosmetics) says: "While clothes may not make the woman, they certainly have a strong effect on her self-confidence – which, I believe, does make the woman."

"Nothing succeeds like the appearance of success."
— Christopher Lasch

"What you see is what you get."
— Flip Wilson

Love: The best motivation

The real sustaining power to keep you going is love. When you love people, you just *have* to show them how they can feel better and be healthier. Can you imagine a finer motivation?

Bonnie feels this way: "Love the people and be very concerned with other people's feelings. If we love people, we have the right attitude to be in the people business. As you help them get what they want, they will help you get what you want. Treat each other like family and like you want to be treated. It works – it's tried and tested."

"It's motive alone that gives character to the actions of men."
— Jean de la Bruyere

"When we talk to our fellow men and they tell us about their troubles, we will listen to them carefully if we have love for them. We will have compassion for their suffering and pain, for we are God's creatures; we are a manifestation of the love of God."
— Elder Thaddeus of Vitovnica

Zest for life

They know you're dead when you quit moving. Zest for life is the joyous energy that keeps us moving, playing and working. If that were to go away, we would start losing mental and muscle tone rapidly.

Zest for life is infectious. It is a gift that you automatically share with everyone you meet. People like to be near you when you have infectious enthusiasm.

The sense of optimism that you bring to your life and work increases your chances of success in any endeavor. Your optimistic zest for life contributes to your health and ability to deal with stressful situations.

> "I am only one, but still I am one; I cannot do everything, but still I can do something; I will not refuse to do the something I can do."
> — Helen Keller

> "A joyful heart is the inevitable result of a heart burning with love."
> — Mother Teresa

Section 8 — A Guide to Learning

Learning is a never-ending process of personal change

Part of the joy of life is the continuous wonder of learning new things. When you integrate new knowledge with what you already know, you build a deep, richly-textured fabric of wisdom that can be applied to make life more satisfying and productive. In other words: knowledge is your key to success.

It's surprising how many people lose the ambition to keep on learning once they finish formal schooling. The fact is that while school (including college) teaches you *how* to learn, most formal education only gives you an initial load of facts and skills. There is so much more to learn as you recognize connections in life, refine your understanding and develop growing wisdom.

A Manager in Louisiana says, "I'll be learning until I'm 90 years old and on crutches." She understands that learning doesn't have to end until the end.

"All human beings, by nature, desire to know."
— Aristotle

"Anyone who stops learning is old, whether twenty or eighty. Anyone who keeps learning today is young. The greatest thing in life is to keep your mind young."
— Henry Ford

"The only person who is educated is the one who has learned how to learn ... and change."
— Carl Rogers

"In a world that is constantly changing, there is no one subject or set of subjects that will serve you for the foreseeable future, let alone for the rest of your life. The most important skill to acquire now is learning how to learn."
— John Naisbitt

"... in the world of the future, the new illiterate will be the person who has not learned how to learn."
— Alvin Toffler

"Knowledge has three degrees – opinion, science, illumination. The means or instrument of the first is sense; of the second, dialectic; of the third, intuition."
— Plotinus

A brief thank you to my readers:

"To read a writer is for me not merely to get an idea of what he says, but to go off with him, and travel in his company."
— Andre Gide (1903)

Imitate what works for others

Look for successful people and learn from what they are doing. When you imitate what they are doing, you can expect to begin having similar results.

Try to not fixate on a single individual. You can do better. Pay attention to the attitudes and results of all the successful people you admire. Fortunately for you, you are in a network organization which, by nature, brings successful people together for mutual support in achieving common goals.

You can meet many of these folks in person and even more through the books they have written. Not every book contains advice that is right for you. But, as you continue reading widely, you will see patterns emerge and begin to identify the things that you change to improve your life.

"Imitation is not just the sincerest form of flattery - it's the sincerest form of learning."
— George Bernard Shaw

Now comes the hard part. You have to actually change. When you recognize old patterns of response that aren't serving you well, work to make that change as quickly and as well as you can. Our habits and mental patterns are real and have power. If you are going to get out of a rut, you have to invest enough energy to get fully clear of it.

Once you have made the desired change, you can see further, broader and more clearly than when you were in a rut. Now is always a good time to take a good look around and reevaluate everything, Fix your sights on your goals. Decide which changes will take you further in the direction of your dreams. Become the agent of your own growth. Nurture yourself.

"I invent nothing; I rediscover."
Rodin

Don't be limited by what others do

When you read a self-help book you can pick up some good ideas. Never, never, stop there. I don't know everything; read other authors. Feed your mind a flood of vicarious experiences. Expose yourself to a wide variety of real experiences. Collect ideas.

Then what do you do next? Have respect for your own experience and good sense. Pick out the changes that are good for you. Send problems to your subconscious to figure out and then listen when creative ideas come back. In the final analysis it's your life; you make choices and you stand responsible for the results.

"If you see in any given situation only what everybody else can see, you can be said to be so much a representative of your culture that you are a victim of it."
— S. I. Hayakawa

"We can be knowledgeable with another man's knowledge, but we cannot be wise with another man's wisdom."
— Michel De Montaigne

Everybody starts out ignorant

It's OK to not know as much as someone else. At one time, that other person knew less than you do now. Do you get the point? You will learn if you persist. Moreover, you can teach what you *do* already know. There are plenty of people who haven't yet opened their eyes to begin to see even the outline of what you already recognize as wonderful and important.

You don't have to have everything figured out before you start. Like a journey, you don't have to know every step ahead of time, just be willing to keep getting closer to your destination. You will learn as you go. You will experiment. You will make mistakes and learn from those mistakes. In the end, you will be the expert that you are hoping to become. People will come to *you* for advice and direction.

"The work will teach you how to do it."
— Estonian Proverb

"To know that you do not know is best. To pretend to know when you do not know is a disease."
— Lao Tzu

"Everyone is ignorant, only in different subjects."
— Will Rogers

Build a library and read
at least one book every month

You are going to accumulate books, eBooks, magazines, Internet links, handouts, notes and clippings. All you have to do is organize your educational materials and you have a library. You should constantly be acquiring more knowledge about your areas of interest. In turn, this should constantly expand your areas of interest.

> "Write to be understood, speak to be heard, read to grow."
> — Lawrence Clark Powell

I'm a tech early-adaptor, but still feel that physical books are the best way to read comfortably and learn at your own pace. On the other hand, the Internet is such a rich source of easily-searchable (and free) information, you should also be comfortable and proficient with your computer.

Building a library shows your commitment to your own education. It provides the means to help others to learn as well. You can recommend your books, read from them at training meetings and even loan them out. But beware; you have been warned:

> "Never loan a book to someone if you expect to get it back. Loaning books is the same as giving them away."
> — Doug Copeland

> "Never lend books, for no one ever returns them; the only books I have in my library are books that other folks have lent me."
> — Anatole France

Set aside a budget for building your library. Subscribe to

appropriate magazines and newsletters. Find books that add important information to your reference collection.

You don't always have to buy books at retail. You can find real bargains in used book stores. If you have a store and you sell books, your wholesaler will save you about 40% off the retail cost. I subscribe to Amazon Prime and am able to enjoy reduced prices and free shipping, even on single copies.

> "Self-education is, I firmly believe, the only kind of education there is."
> — Isaac Asimov

> "Nothing has such power to broaden the mind as the ability to investigate systematically and truly all that comes under thy observation in life."
> — Marcus Aurelius

> "A man may know himself by the books he keeps."
> — Ronan Graybear

Learning and teaching

Studying and learning earns many long-term benefits. It improves your self-confidence because you become recognizably more knowledgeable and competent. You are aware that you know more, and so does everyone else. Your reputation will grow.

Studying and learning sets you apart. Not everyone has the self-discipline to apply themselves persistently. It's amazing how many people do just enough to get by.

> "The best thing for being sad," replied Merlin, beginning to puff and blow, "is to learn something. That's the only thing

that never fails. You may grow old and trembling in your anatomies, you may lie awake at night listening to the disorder of your veins, you may miss your only love, you may see the world about you devastated by evil lunatics, or know your honour trampled in the sewers of baser minds. There is only one thing for it then — to learn. Learn why the world wags and what wags it. That is the only thing which the mind can never exhaust, never alienate, never be tortured by, never fear or distrust, and never dream of regretting. Learning is the only thing for you. Look what a lot of things there are to learn."
— T.H. White, *The Once and Future King*

Studying and learning makes you a better teacher. Teaching, in turn, reinforces what you have learned. You will make many close friends because your students will appreciate your sharing your knowledge with them. Teaching and, especially, mentoring are very personal activities that bond people together.

When your customers have questions and you have answers, this strengthens your position in the marketplace. Your reputation will spread and the extra word-of-mouth advertising will increase your business.

"If you want to build a ship, don't drum up people together to collect wood and don't assign them tasks and work, but rather teach them to long for the endless immensity of the sea."
— Antoine de Saint-Exupéry

"True teachers are those who use themselves as bridges over which they invite their students to cross; then, having facilitated their crossing, joyfully collapse, encouraging them to create their
own."
— Nikos Kazantzakis

Section 9 — Exerting Influence and Gaining Compliance

Our predictable social responses

As "social animals" we are responsive to certain common preconceived notions and powerful trigger situations. Our reflex reactions are very predictable. They form the necessary fabric of our society. We are taught, and often disciplined, to respect authority, conserve valuable resources, make friends and protect the helpless.

For some of us it may be shocking to realize how much advertising is crafted to motivate us, and how much of what we say to others pushes their social reflexes. On the other hand, it's good to be aware of such influences. Awareness means that we can be in better control of how we respond, and that we can be less callous or clumsy in how we treat others.

> "Advertising has us working jobs we don't like so that we can buy stuff we don't need to impress people we don't know."
> — Ronan Graybear

Don't be cynical about it, but people can be influenced. We behave in predictable ways. This is a normal part of our civilized behavior. We teach, sell and negotiate in every facet of our lives. When we think that we are right, we try to get our way or persuade others to our point of view.

It's not inherently bad to understand human reactions and apply that understanding. The evil is to use our knowledge of influence to move someone away from their own best interests.

> "If you treat people right, they will treat you right — ninety percent of the time."
> — Franklin D. Roosevelt

The purposes of communication

Sometimes you communicate just to share information or entertain. But, more often than not, you are trying to influence someone to achieve your desired outcome. Face it, you are trying to change someone's attitude or behavior. Do you have the right to do that?

Look at this question from another point of view. What is the point of any communication if there is not a goal or desired outcome? Such a conversation would be as pointless (and probably as uninteresting) as a journey with no destination.

You have things to share with others. You have a unique background that combines your inborn characteristics with your personal experiences. You know things that are interesting. You have information that may be valuable to others.

When you have strong emotions about something, the ability to express yourself clearly, with kindness and humor, will help your contribution be welcomed in a conversation. It's okay to be you and express yourself to others. It's okay to influence someone to your way of thinking or to make things come out the way you want if you play fair. Remember, "influence" is not the same as "manipulate."

Do you have the others' best interests at heart? Are you telling the truth? Are you alert to the other person's response? Are you flexible? Are you consistent? Does your desired outcome dovetail with what the other person wants or needs?

Stimulating positive results

Have you noticed that some people have trouble learning from a book? They may learn more-easily when someone explains things to them or if they learn by doing. Not everyone experiences the world in the same way you do. Different learning styles affect some people more profoundly than others.

Auditory people respond better to what they HEAR. Visual people respond better to what they SEE. Kinesthetic people respond better to what they DO and FEEL. Everybody responds better to a positive goal. (These statements represent tendencies, not absolutes.)

When you recognize how the person you're communicating with learns and responds, you can do a better job of engaging them. When they imagine the end results you want to achieve, what are they hearing, seeing and feeling? If you are communicating well, they will have a clear and positive impression of your desired outcome.

Backtrack a minute. Before you can share your goal, you have to understand it clearly yourself. Take some quiet time to imagine how things will be when you achieve what you want. See how that looks. Hear how success will sound. Feel how you hope to feel. You need all of this. If you get "off the track," come back to this moment and choose more clearly the best way to achieve your goal.

Making Commitments: "CoudjaWoudjaWhen"

My aunt, Joy Marshall, taught me that the mind has several necessary, progressive stages that must be experienced in order to make commitments. Of course, she uses this to motivate herself and others. Joy also uses this technique for emotional healing therapy. It is especially helpful when a person needs to recognize and commit to release specific negative emotions.

Could You? First, you have to acknowledge that the change is possible.

Would You? Next, you have to acknowledge that you would be willing to make the change.

When? Finally, you have to commit to actually doing it.

This is a very powerful technique. In the case of old resentments, for instance, once you've said "yes" to the first two questions, your mind knows that the answer to the third is "right now." Then, the anger just melts away leaving you feeling all clean and shaky.

I think the principle holds true for all kinds of decision and commitment making. This is well worth exploring.

What gets rewarded gets done

Why do something if nobody notices or cares? Measurement permits recognition, which is necessary before there can be a reward. Notice the many ways that you respond to the offer of a reward and how you might use similar measurements and rewards to motivate others.

Unfortunately, this concept can also be used for ill. If a situation is set up to measure or reward the wrong intention or action, the wrong thing will get done. For instance, when I worked in a computer support group, our new boss decided to rank us according to the number of problem reports that we cleared each week. The result was that lazy technicians chose the easy problems. Some workers prematurely reported problems as closed. This forced the person with a problem to call in a "new" report to get anything done.

Not every person will respond to such external rewards or threats. I didn't like my boss's problem-reporting game and wouldn't play; I enjoyed the personal challenge (including the praise, recognition and reputation among the clients) of solving the tough problems. My new boss never understood what pushed my buttons, but he did build an impressive rank-reporting database system that got him promoted. I see now that he was simply manipulating the measures for which *he* was being evaluated.

Network marketing organizations are notorious for measuring your sales and recruiting activity and offering rewards. Our cats will almost always chase a little ball that we bounce their way. But, you don't have to respond to every carrot or stick. Decide which trips or bonuses you want to achieve and then have the dignity to ignore whatever rah-rah is not important to you.

On the other hand, rewards are actually quite effective for many people. You probably should consider organizing contests and prizes for achievement among the people in your organization. Hey, make it fun. Try not to be too cynical.

Price is associated with quality

We have come to accept and expect that something has more value if we have to work harder or sacrifice more to acquire it. This is expressed in sayings such as "You get what you pay for," and "You have to pay for quality."

A seller of tourist jewelry noticed that one rack was moving slowly and left a note for a clerk to re-price it by half. Misreading the note the clerk doubled the prices instead. It didn't take long for customers to buy most of the rack. The owner learned a valuable lesson.

There are several take-away: 1) If you give things away (such as third-party literature or nutritional consultations) people will not fully respect their value. 2) Stick with the marketing plan. Once you start selling retail at membership rates, people will have no motivation to let you sponsor them.

Coupons mean a discount

We all know people who collect, file, organize and trade coupons. They save a lot of money. We may envy them. The fact is that not every coupon is valuable to every person. What do you save if you buy something at discount if you don't need that item? Worse, merchants have discovered that some people respond to a coupon even when it does not offer a real discount.

And, of course, now that you are now the seller, it would make sense to pay attention to coupons in your own marketing.

It's easier to believe the experts

We cannot know everything. In an increasingly complicated world, it is increasingly necessary to accept the judgment of strong authorities for guidance. Actually, even weak authorities will often do.

Most people will not have the interest or resources to do their own searches in the scientific literature. In fact, many people will simply ask a friend or neighbor where they buy their auto insurance rather than to do their own comparison shopping. I'm not being entirely critical here; the tendency to take this kind of shortcut is a hardwired default in our brains.

Some "authoritarian" cultures are particularly strong on listening exclusively to the "trusted authorities" of their own group. In other cultures, each person is expected to more-personally own the things they believe.

I don't have any strong suggestions or judgments for you here; I just thought it should be included for your consideration.

Evaluating relative differences

When I bought a home several years ago, the real estate agent, right away, showed us several homes she knew we couldn't afford. When she showed us homes closer to our price range, they suddenly seemed more affordable.

We may be reluctant to make a large commitment at first, but be willing to make additional smaller commitments. Try this experiment. Fill three buckets; one each with tolerable hot, cold and room-temperature water. Put one hand in the hot and one hand in the cold and wait a few minutes to get used to the extremes. Now put both hands in the room-temperature water. You'll be surprised at how differently your hands interpret the same water.

Salesmen use the same principle when they sell the most expensive part of a wardrobe or program first. After investing heavily, a customer is more willing to pay for accessories. When my family took a multi-day tour, we were reluctant to sign-up ahead of time for side-trips. We were easier to convince later, during the trip, when the extra seemed so much less, in contrast to the cost of the full tour.

When a restaurant asks, "would you like fries with that" they are using the same principal. You will probably end up encouraging distributors to increase their activity to the next threshold, which offers additional benefits. It often works.

We feel obliged to return the favor

When someone does you a favor, you feel the urge to return the favor. That is why, when you ask a favor, after having done something for someone, it is very hard for them to refuse.

Have you ever been in a public place and had someone press

a flower, card or gift into your hand and then request a small donation? Even if you refused, I'll bet it took an effort to suppress the reaction to comply. Not only do we feel social obligations to give generously and repay gifts, we also feel an obligation to receive whatever gift is offered, especially when we are surprised.

In the same way, free samples trigger the urge to buy whatever you've tried. We frequently return from the grocery store with packages of foods that we agreed to sample while shopping. If your organization makes samples available, they can be surprisingly effective. Remember to follow up by directly asking for an order.

Negotiating

We often feel the need to make concessions to others who make concessions to us. This is the core of the negotiating advice, "Always ask for more than you want." People will feel more inclined to meet your request after you have agreed to "compromise."

Once you have agreed to do something (such as volunteer work) you are more likely to agree to do it again. Not only that, but you will feel some responsibility to do it again and feel satisfied with the arrangement! Of course, if the initial demand is too extreme, the bargaining is not in good faith and the tactic will backfire.

As with everything else in this book, these comments are meant to be food for thought. For instance, a little additional effort will reveal complete books on negotiating. When you are ready, you can dive in deeper.

We feel committed to our choices

Once we make a choice, we have a strong desire to appear consistent with that choice. Even very small concessions can lead to progressively large commitments. We will do everything possible to justify our choice. No one wants to be seen as indecisive, scatterbrained or weak-willed. So, sticking to a choice helps us avoid having to re-evaluating that choice.

As an example, if you gave to a charity, you would be more likely to agree to collect for that charity on your block. This is the core of the "foot in the door" principle. Once you agree to a trivial request or make an initial purchase, your need to be consistent will influence you to agree to larger requests or to buy more-expensive related items. When our boys were young, they asked for, and we bought them, a small box of Lego® building blocks. From that point on, we found it almost impossible to say no to a request for more Lego® sets. We even took pride in seeking out the latest variations. Good work, guys.

Consistency is not inherently bad. People quote Ralph Waldo Emerson as saying "Consistency is the hobgoblin of little minds." What he actually said was "A *foolish* consistency is the hobgoblin of little minds." Keep doing something that is working well or experiment with something else. It's your call.

We value what we have to fight for

Active public commitments such as offering testimonials or signing a pledge are some of the strongest motivators. For instance, if you write down a goal you are more likely to pursue it. If you show people your written goal you are even more likely to achieve it.

The more effort you put into a commitment, the more power

it has. This is why initiation rituals (such as armed forces boot camps) are so effective at generating loyalty to organizations. If you have to fight for something you will value it more highly. I have a ratty old sweater that my wife keeps trying to throw out. I never wear it but I've made such an issue of keeping it that, now, I just can't bear to let it go.

The strongest commitments are those we make on our own by taking inner responsibility. The key is believing that we want to because of our own convictions, rather than because of outside pressure.

If everybody is doing it, it must be right

We feel a social responsibility to conform to group standards. It's hard to stand out as different. When there is a group present and you are uncertain, you will look to others for behavioral clues.

As an example, when I first started promoting my herb business I discovered a traffic location where cars backed up for a quarter mile on weekends. I printed a pile of flyers and went there to hand them out. Usually everything went well as my smile and I strode confidently from one driver to the next.

Drivers could watch me working my way up to them. People in the next car would usually roll their window down, accept my flyer and smile back. When I reached a fearful or grumpy driver, however, I discovered that the next driver was much less likely to take my flyer. It was time to turn around, walk back and wait for that group of cars to drive past the light.

We are very vulnerable to the influence of those we associate with. Children who are afraid of dogs lose their fear when shown films where variety of other children are having fun with dogs. On the other hand, "bad associations spoil useful habits."

Children become more aggressive when they watch films of people intentionally harming others. The powers of peer pressure on people of all ages are well known.

Many people will sing silly songs, stand on chairs, or donate cash if everybody else is doing it.

The power of direct command

If someone is uncertain they will hesitate. If you give a direct command, they will often comply. At an accident don't just cry, "Won't somebody please do something!" Point at a specific person and say: "You. Go call an ambulance."

The typical routine for handling a product demonstration involves giving some very specific guidance to the hostess. You explain the routine of introducing you and passing around the sign-in sheet. (That's another example. You just tell everyone to make an entry for themselves and they usually do.)

Afterwards you have the previous hostess go with you to the next presentation sponsored by her friend and say a few words. Before long, she is giving her own presentations and training her own people. No muss, no fuss. It's just how things are done.

When we switched away from accepting checks for phone orders, we discovered that the best way to handle the situation was to not raise the issue. Now we just ask which credit card will be used. This combines an indirect command ("use a credit card") with the opportunity to make a choice. Frankly, it works very well.

Studies have shown that 95% of people are basically imitators (followers) and that only 5% are initiators (leaders). When a follower is not sure what to do next, they are very open to the influence of their group and especially to the group leader... or even someone who just seems very sure of themselves.

Everyone likes to be liked

It's hard to resist when a friend asks you to do something. By extension, it's even hard to resist a stranger who seems to be likable (such as a Girl Scout with a smile and cookies).

People who look good automatically seem more honest, kind and intelligent. This goes double for tall men and pretty girls. Those of us who are funny-looking, bald and squeaky-voiced simply have to work harder to make a good impression. Happily, when people do decide to like me, it's easier to believe that it's not just my stunning hair and dazzling smile.

It is also easier for people to like others who seem familiar or are similar to themselves. (Happily, working together for a common purpose builds familiarity.) It helps if you are the same age, have the same background or dress the same way. It's a smart move to subtly imitate the body postures and speaking rhythms of someone if you want them to like you a little better.

I like to be liked. I'll really go out of my way to please someone who really appreciates my efforts. When someone is grumpy, demanding and unappreciative, I just can't seem to get as excited. Somehow I expect my labors will turn into another instance of "no good deed goes unpunished."

We tend to believe compliments and especially love to hear ourselves being praised to a third party. Don't hesitate to be an encouraging person who is quick to offer positive comments.

If you tend to complain or be critical, do everything in your power to stop that behavior. Complaining represents the combination of anger and impotence (lack of control). Neither of these are not attractive or constructive to yourself or others.

Also, as my wife, Dianna, has pointed out, "it takes at least seven positive things to counter any negative thing that you say." Dianna was still an elementary school teacher at the time.

She practiced this principal every day and it is no wonder that her students adored her. She mentioned this after I made a critical comment to her. She demanded that I immediately produce seven positive comments. I like to think that I have been more positive ever since.

> "A beautiful thing happens when we start paying attention to each other. It is by participating more in your relationship that you breathe life into it."
> — Steve Maraboli, *Unapologetically You: Reflections on Life and the Human Experience*

Compulsive response to authority

We have all been trained to color within the lines, do what the teacher says and obey policemen. We will often do what the boss wants even if we dislike doing it.

This normally useful response can become our most frightening social reflex. Strong leaders and governmental authorities have used their power of authority to influence armies and ordinary citizens to perform hideous atrocities against others and even voluntarily commit suicide. Think of Hitler, Jim Jones and terrorist organizations.

Part of the reason for the influence of authority (or even the appearance of authority) is our assumption that they know more than we do. Another aspect is their control of our rewards and punishment. Authoritarianism is also a natural psycho-social stage of development.

Bob Altemeyer, a psychologist, conducted decades of research that made him an established expert on authoritarianism. His book, *The Authoritarians* can be found online as a free PDF file if you are interested in learning more.

A practical example of mechanical, blind obedience to authority is the medical establishment. People routinely sign a release statement when entering a hospital (even for minor, non-invasive tests) that basically says that the doctors may do whatever they want to you. This is a mirror of the blind faith of generations of patients who meekly (and ignorantly) accepted whatever drugs or surgeries were prescribed (including bleeding and administration of mercury). Hospital staffs are subject to a long tradition of submission to doctors' orders.

Get it while you can

"This is your last chance. If you act soon and for a limited time only, while supply lasts, and if your entry is drawn, you can be one of the exclusive few to win a rare original."

It's easy to assume that if something is difficult to get, it is more valuable. We will camp out in a ticket line, pay extra for signed and numbered limited editions and inventory close-out sales. I love auctions and liquidation sales. I'll buy stuff I don't need. What if I want it later and I can't get it?

Also, for what it's worth, we hate to lose our freedom of choice. When information is censored or hard to get, it can seem more persuasive.

Because there is a reason

You ask someone to do something. They hesitate. You say "because" and tell them why they should. They agree to do it. This doesn't just work with very small children. What happened? It may be more than your persuasive argument. "Everything has to have a reason" and people are influenced simply because there *is* a reason. Researchers have discovered that many people will comply if you use the word "because," even *without* a reason. It's kind of scary.

The best defenses against exploitation

The best way to protect yourself against being manipulated by these social triggers is two-fold. You must be aware of these methods and you must be aware of your gut feelings. When you notice that something feels wrong, stop in your tracks and refuse to respond further until you have figured out what is going on.

Are you vulnerable? Are you stressed, distracted, tired or rushed? If you are, you are more likely to make these automatic shortcuts to decision-making. These days we are assaulted by more information and are under pressure to do more in less time. Knowledge is growing explosively and access to that knowledge is growing even faster. We can communicate instantly and have many times the choices of earlier generations. We get used to making snap decisions based on minimal direct evidence.

When you notice that funny feeling in your stomach and realize that you are becoming emotionally involved in a decision, stop to decide why. Someone may be pushing your triggers. This might actually be a good thing. In this fast-paced world we need shortcuts for decision-making. But when someone falsely misrepresents the facts to get your compliance, it's okay to "JUST SAY NO."

Creating change

People tend to resist change. They are used to old patterns and relationships and can feel threatened. Their negative emotional responses can make it hard to create change even when it is obviously in their best interest. Here are techniques to help:

Create a vacuum — "Nature abhors a vacuum." So does human nature. Dismantle or discard the old system. This makes physical or logical room for the new.

When we needed to move our shipping department to the store, I took the initiative to remove everything from the new space that would be used. That made it easier for my staff to "fill the hole."

The same thing works when you need to clean up and get organized. I find that the first thing to do is throw out all the stuff that can be discarded. Next, you take out all the stuff that doesn't belong; it should go somewhere else. By that time, there is usually enough empty space to begin organizing items that need to stay.

Create the initial framework yourself — Leaders need to express their vision. If you do enough of the preliminary work for others to see and understand where you're going, it is easier to delegate the completion of the work. Your people will feel like they're stepping on rocks rather than wading through mud.

In my engineering work, I sometimes needed to collect information from others. It could be like pulling teeth. I discovered that, if I preprinted the forms with the information that was already known, people were much more willing to make corrections or add missing information. Don't we all hate going to a professional service provider and being asked to provide information redundantly on multiple forms – especially when you know that they already have most of it on their computers. We wouldn't do it if we didn't feel like we simply had to.

Perhaps you want to ask your managers to start sending out

their own monthly newsletters or you want distributors to be more comfortable holding meetings. If you supply the initial framework to get them started, it will be easier for them to get past the "inventing the wheel" stage. Give them a copy of your word processing template, ready for them to fill in the empty spaces. Provide a demonstration kit or at least lists, sample forms and a speaking outline.

Create an artificial crisis — If you just have to get something moving, cause an emergency. People will work hard to get things back under control even if that requires accepting a changed situation. If your teenager won't take his dirty clothes to the laundry, just let clothes accumulate until he has nothing clean to wear. When this artificial crisis finally gets his attention, you can persuade him to begin washing his own clothes. Of course, he can create his own crisis by doing it so badly that you decide to go back to doing it yourself. Some ideas do backfire.

Managing change

Resistance to change is normal and can even be positive; it shows that people are involved and care about the situation. Listen sincerely to objections. Just letting people express their feelings can diffuse resistance. However, their challenges might also lead to improvements to the original plan. The resulting dialogue can improve communication and cooperation.

Communicate — Help people understand why you have decided on the change. Fear, uncertainty and doubt (the "FUD" factor) can be quickly neutralized by your courtesy of explaining the needs and benefits that led to your decision.

Involve others — People will usually support a change that they've helped to plan and execute. Why should you do all the work just to run into a brick wall?

Plant the idea and cultivate it — Try to avoid ramming a change down someone else's throat. It you start early, and are patient, you can actually plant and direct the gradual development of your idea so that others think that it is their own. Then, when they "own" the desire to change, it is much easier to let them run with it and adjust their direction slightly as needed. Who says there isn't a little Sun Tzu or Machiavelli in us all?

Rewards and benefits — Everyone affected by a change needs to feel that there's "something in it" for them. If they don't, maybe it's a bad move and really should be resisted. The timing may be off or it may actually create additional burdens without sufficient benefits.

p.s. "Change happens."

Section 10 — Doing Business from Home

It just took over the house

In the Oct/Nov '92 issue of *Sunshine Horizons*, Beverly Lewis tells about "one couple so committed to this business they've literally turned their entire house into a miniature university. As I walked through their kitchen during a visit one day, I saw a Nature's Spring [company brand of water filter] on the counter. The kitchen table was loaded with company products and literature. Each of the rooms was filled with educational books and other related paraphernalia. After touring their home and noticing no bedroom, I couldn't help ask them where they sleep! Their level of enthusiasm amazes me, and it's just one example. There are thousands of others."

Each person must decide how they want to deal with this problem as it happens. You can set firm limits, throttle the business to keep it from growing further, move, add room or open a store. Your choice should meet your needs for room, privacy, location and potential for further expansion.

> "Blessed is he who has found his work. Let him ask no other blessing."
> — Thomas Carlyle

> "Be careful what you ask for, you might get it."
> — Mr. Spock

When there's nowhere to hide

Sometimes you just need to wash dishes, read a book or shave your legs. If your business is in your house, people will drop by at unpredictable times. When the business is small, that might not be such a problem. In fact, being available to care and share at odd hours may be a valuable service that distinguishes you from less-popular competitors. But, setting limits may save your sanity.

Setting (and enforcing) business hours

One way to manage the demands on your time is to post the hours that you are open and then stick to them. It's not always easy to be firm when a friend with a need (but poor planning skills) knows that you must be in the house somewhere – and you forgot to lock the back door. It's usually not that bad. Most people will respect your need to have an orderly life with some time set aside for sleep or whimpering in a corner.

Less TV, more real life

Soap operas, reruns and especially the hot new shows can sap your time and attention. TV can be entertaining, but building a new business can be a lot more fun. Instead of watching other people do things and listening to other people laugh, you can enjoy the real thing.

> "This time, like all times, is a very good one, if we but know what to do with it.
> — Emerson

> "Television watching takes up more time than any other activity our society engages in."
> — *Scientific Australian*

> "The whole day stretches before us with unlimited opportunity! And what better way to appreciate that opportunity than by squandering it watching cartoons all day!"
> — Calvin, *Weirdos from Another Planet*, Bill Watterson

Bottles behind the bushes

As much as you would like to spend all your time waiting for people to show up and pick up their products, there *are* some other things that need to be done from time to time.

I solved the problem by telling customers how much their check should be and then leaving their products, invoice and an envelope in a dry spot on the porch. They picked up their herbs, put their check in the envelope and shoved it through a crack in the garage door. It worked like a charm.

One loyal customer was a real estate agent who couldn't spare the time during the day and liked to drop by after 10:30 p.m. Bottles behind the bushes made us both very happy; she got her herbs and we got our sleep.

Don't forget your family

Take time to be with your family. A new business can be demanding but it doesn't deserve your total attention. You probably started the business to help your family with their health or finances. Trading your income for your time, attention and love makes a lousy exchange.

Be kind to your family. Don't let your anxiety or frustrations with business matters carry over to your spouse and children; you will need their support and good will at times like these.

When you set a goal, take the wishes and circumstances of your family into consideration. Don't leave them behind. In fact, it's a good idea to involve your family in planning and decision making. They will often think of things you might have overlooked. Their input can be invaluable.

Your family may even enjoy participating in the business. Because "opposites attract" it's likely that your spouse has qualities that will complement yours. Split up the responsibilities in a way that makes the best use of individual talents. Very few people have achieved business success without the support of their family.

When you outgrow the house

After a while, the business may be just too big to keep on running from your house. My sponsors kept on cannibalizing their home until they had to move out and buy the house next door to live in.

I lived in a sub-division with deed restrictions. Once I moved all the herbs to a store, I could finally relax about not offending my neighbors with frequent traffic.

Actually, zoning ordinances can be a blessing in disguise. A past "Manager of the Year" team admits that they took a leap of faith and opened a store even though they weren't financially ready to move. Once all their eggs were in one basket, they just had to succeed.

About the time you have developed five to ten managers, you will be faced with a decision about your retail sales. Do you deliberately cut back and send people to your successline, or do you make a separate place for the business? This is a very individual question and no other person's decision will be exactly right for you.

How does your approach to business fit with your house? Do you prefer giving home demonstrations? Do you need more privacy, more room or a better location? This is one of those major forks in the road. Meditate carefully on your choice; it can have permanent effects.

Gratitude to the reader — and a request

YOU are a vital part of marketing for a new generation of self-published authors. *Thank you for buying and reading this book!* And, if you would be so kind, **please let others know** that you enjoyed this book and why you recommend it to them. This is how much of publishing works now. Thank you, thank you, thank you.

This book was self-published using the resources of *CreateSpace*. It could not have been completed and marketed without modern web-based technology. And, this old fart loves tech. Thank you to all the optimistic techies out there. Have you hugged your nerd today?

Special thanks to **Dianna Satterlee**, my wife. Di is a bright soul, the light of my heart, a retired teacher, gifted cook and special friend. She has made the lives of many, many people better for her being in this world. She is also the secret sauce in my recipe for writing, and has inspired, cooperated, facilitated and participated in many ways.

I am also publishing a book of essays and a book of short stories in parallel with this business guide. I invite you to also enjoy these additional writing efforts.

Please consider following my thoughts and scribbles at:

SocioDynamics.org
@ChumForThought
facebook.com/david.satterlee

You have reached the end of this book, but your future stands poised to enter a bright day. My best wishes to you, your family and your vibrant, growing network.

www.ingramcontent.com/pod-product-compliance
Lightning Source LLC
Chambersburg PA
CBHW051338170526
45166CB00002B/868